PRINCEWILL LAGANG

Divine Dating: A Christian Perspective on Finding Love

First published by PRINCEWILL LAGANG 2023

Copyright © 2023 by Princewill Lagang

All rights reserved. No part of this publication may be reproduced, stored or transmitted in any form or by any means, electronic, mechanical, photocopying, recording, scanning, or otherwise without written permission from the publisher. It is illegal to copy this book, post it to a website, or distribute it by any other means without permission.

Princewill Lagang asserts the moral right to be identified as the author of this work.

First edition

This book was professionally typeset on Reedsy.
Find out more at reedsy.com

Contents

1	The Quest for Love	1
2	Faith as Your Compass	4
3	The Art of Connection	7
4	Navigating Challenges and Staying True to Faith	10
5	Cultivating Love and Commitment	13
6	The Decision to Commit	16
7	Nurturing Lasting Love	19
8	Love that Endures	22
9	A Love that Transcends	25
10	A Love That Inspires	28
11	A Future Filled with Faith and Love	31
12	A Love That Endures Eternally	34

1

The Quest for Love

Introduction

- Opening Quote: "Love is patient, love is kind..." – 1 Corinthians 13:4-7
- Setting the Stage: Introduce the concept of dating and finding love from a Christian perspective. Explain that this book aims to provide guidance and insights into building meaningful, loving relationships rooted in faith.

Section 1: The Modern Dating Landscape

- Defining Dating: Explain the contemporary understanding of dating, its challenges, and how it has evolved over the years.
- The Digital Age: Discuss the impact of technology and dating apps on modern relationships.
- Cultural Influences: Highlight how popular culture and societal norms shape dating behavior.

Section 2: The Christian Approach to Love

- Biblical Foundation: Explore the Christian perspective on love as described in the Bible, emphasizing the love of God and the command to love others.

- Christian Values: Discuss the importance of faith, purity, and commitment in Christian relationships.

- Seeking God's Will: Emphasize the idea of seeking God's guidance in finding a life partner.

Section 3: The Purpose of Dating

- God's Plan for Love: Explain how dating can be a means to fulfilling God's plan for love and partnership.

- Preparing for Marriage: Discuss the role of dating in discerning compatibility for a lifelong commitment.

- Developing Character: Emphasize how dating can help individuals grow in character and faith.

Section 4: Challenges and Misconceptions

- Common Challenges: Address some common obstacles faced by Christians in the dating world, such as peer pressure and temptation.

- Myths and Misconceptions: Debunk popular myths about Christian dating, such as the idea that it's all about waiting for "the one."

Section 5: Your Dating Journey Begins

- Self-Reflection: Encourage readers to start their dating journey with introspection, understanding their values, desires, and goals.

- Setting Boundaries: Discuss the importance of setting healthy boundaries in dating, especially in terms of physical intimacy and communication.

- Prayer and Patience: Stress the role of prayer and patience in the dating process.

Section 6: What to Expect in This Book

- Outline of the Book: Give an overview of the upcoming chapters and what readers can expect to learn.
  - Closing Thoughts: Reiterate the central message of the book: that divine dating is a path to finding love guided by Christian principles.

Closing

- Final Thoughts: End the chapter with a hopeful and inspiring message about the potential for finding love in a way that aligns with one's faith.
  - Reflection Questions: Provide a set of reflection questions for readers to contemplate and discuss, preparing them for the journey ahead.

This detailed outline for Chapter 1, "The Quest for Love," sets the stage for the book "Divine Dating: A Christian Perspective on Finding Love" and introduces the core themes and concepts that will be explored in subsequent chapters.

2

Faith as Your Compass

Introduction

- Opening Quote: "Trust in the Lord with all your heart and lean not on your own understanding." – Proverbs 3:5

- Recap of Chapter 1: Briefly summarize the key points from Chapter 1, emphasizing the importance of aligning your dating journey with your Christian faith.

Section 1: The Role of Faith in Dating

- Faith-Centered Dating: Explain the significance of placing faith at the center of your dating experience. How faith can guide your choices and actions.

- Building on a Strong Foundation: Discuss the idea that a relationship built on shared faith can weather the storms of life more effectively.

Section 2: Prerequisites for a Faith-Centered Relationship

- Self-Examination: Encourage readers to assess their own faith and relationship with God before seeking a partner.

- Spiritual Maturity: Discuss the importance of partnering with someone who shares your level of spiritual maturity.
- Common Values: Highlight the need for shared values and goals within a faith-centered relationship.

Section 3: Discernment in Dating

- The Power of Prayer: Discuss the role of prayer in seeking God's guidance throughout the dating process.
- Listening to Your Heart and God: Explain how to discern whether a potential partner is in alignment with God's plan for your life.
- Red Flags and Deal Breakers: Help readers identify warning signs and non-negotiables that should not be compromised.

Section 4: Navigating Dating Challenges

- Temptations and Challenges: Address common challenges faced by Christians in dating, including the temptation to compromise values.
- Peer Pressure and Social Expectations: Discuss how to handle external pressures from friends and family who may not understand your faith-centered approach.

Section 5: Biblical Models of Love and Relationships

- Biblical Examples: Share stories from the Bible that demonstrate healthy and faith-centered relationships, such as the love story of Ruth and Boaz.
- Lessons from Scripture: Extract valuable lessons from these stories and explain how they can be applied to modern dating.

Section 6: Tools for Faith-Centered Dating

- Accountability Partners: Explain the benefits of having accountability partners who can provide support and guidance.

- Journaling and Reflection: Encourage readers to keep a dating journal to record their thoughts, prayers, and progress.
- Community and Church Involvement: Stress the importance of staying connected with your faith community for support and guidance.

Closing

- Final Thoughts: Summarize the key takeaways from the chapter, emphasizing that faith should be the guiding compass in your dating journey.
- Reflection Questions: Provide a set of reflection questions for readers to ponder and discuss, helping them internalize the lessons from this chapter.

Chapter 2, "Faith as Your Compass," continues to build on the foundation laid in the first chapter, providing readers with practical insights and guidance on integrating faith into their dating experiences. It also addresses the challenges of maintaining a faith-centered approach in the modern dating landscape.

3

The Art of Connection

Introduction
- Opening Quote: "Two are better than one, because they have a good return for their labor." – Ecclesiastes 4:9
- Recap of Previous Chapters: Briefly summarize the key points from Chapters 1 and 2, reinforcing the importance of faith in dating and discernment.

Section 1: Building Meaningful Connections

- The Foundation of Love: Discuss how genuine love is rooted in connection, both with God and with a potential partner.
- Authenticity: Emphasize the importance of being true to oneself and seeking authenticity in a partner.
- Communication: Address the vital role of effective communication in building connections and understanding one another.

Section 2: Finding Like-Minded Individuals

- Shared Interests: Encourage readers to explore common interests and activities that align with their faith and values to meet potential partners.

- Church and Faith-Based Groups: Discuss the benefits of getting involved in church activities and faith-based organizations to connect with like-minded individuals.

- Online Christian Communities: Introduce the idea of using the internet to find Christian dating platforms and communities.

Section 3: The First Meeting - Dating with Purpose

- Defining Intentions: Explain the significance of approaching dating with a clear purpose and intention of building a faith-centered relationship.

- First Impressions: Offer guidance on how to make a positive first impression and share one's faith in a natural and genuine way.

- Planning the Date: Provide suggestions for planning a date that aligns with Christian values and encourages meaningful conversation.

Section 4: Nurturing Connections

- Getting to Know Each Other: Discuss strategies for deepening the connection with a potential partner, including open and honest conversations.

- Shared Faith Discussions: Emphasize the importance of discussing faith, beliefs, and values to ensure alignment.

- Building Trust: Share tips for building trust within the relationship, rooted in Christian principles.

Section 5: Red Flags and Boundaries

- Recognizing Warning Signs: Help readers identify red flags that may indicate an unhealthy or incompatible relationship.

- Setting Boundaries: Discuss the importance of establishing and respecting boundaries in dating, especially in terms of physical intimacy and faith-related matters.

Section 6: Dating as a Process of Discernment

- The Journey of Discernment: Explain how dating is a process of discerning whether a person is the right life partner.
    - Seeking God's Guidance: Encourage readers to continuously seek God's guidance in their dating journey.
    - Being Open to God's Plan: Stress the idea that God's plan may not always align with our own, and that flexibility and trust in His plan are essential.

Closing

- Final Thoughts: Summarize the key takeaways from the chapter, highlighting the importance of building meaningful connections rooted in faith.
    - Reflection Questions: Provide a set of reflection questions for readers to contemplate and discuss, helping them apply the principles of connection and discernment in their dating lives.

Chapter 3, "The Art of Connection," delves into the practical aspects of building meaningful relationships and connections while dating with a Christian perspective. It provides guidance on finding like-minded individuals, planning meaningful dates, and nurturing connections in a way that aligns with faith and values.

4

Navigating Challenges and Staying True to Faith

Introduction

- Opening Quote: "I can do all things through Christ who strengthens me." – Philippians 4:13

- Recap of Previous Chapters: Provide a brief recap of the key concepts discussed in Chapters 1 to 3, emphasizing the importance of faith, connection, and discernment in Christian dating.

Section 1: Common Challenges in Faith-Centered Dating

- Temptation and Peer Pressure: Discuss the challenges of maintaining Christian values in a dating context, including temptations and societal pressures.

- Spiritual Differences: Address the potential difficulties that may arise when dating someone with differing levels of faith or beliefs.

- Long-Distance Relationships: Explore how to navigate challenges that can come with dating someone from a different faith community or geographical location.

Section 2: Overcoming Challenges with Faith

- Prayer and Strength: Emphasize the role of prayer in seeking strength and guidance during challenging times in the dating journey.
    - Community Support: Discuss the importance of turning to your faith community for support and advice when facing difficulties.
    - Staying Grounded in Scripture: Encourage readers to turn to the Bible for wisdom and inspiration when encountering challenges.

Section 3: Staying True to Your Values

- Values and Boundaries: Reiterate the importance of setting and upholding boundaries in alignment with Christian values.
    - The Role of Accountability: Discuss the benefits of having accountability partners who can help you stay true to your values.
    - Honest Conversations: Highlight the significance of open and honest communication with your partner regarding your faith and values.

Section 4: Conflict Resolution and Forgiveness

- Conflict in Relationships: Address the inevitability of conflicts in relationships and provide strategies for resolving them while maintaining Christian values.
    - The Art of Forgiveness: Discuss the role of forgiveness in healing and strengthening relationships, drawing from biblical examples.

Section 5: Navigating Family and Social Dynamics

- Family Support: Offer advice on involving family members in the process and how to address concerns or differences in faith.
    - Friendship and Peer Relationships: Discuss how to manage friendships

and social dynamics when you're dating with a Christian perspective.

Section 6: When Faith Leads to Love

- Success Stories: Share inspirational stories of Christian couples who navigated challenges and found lasting love through their shared faith.
    - Reflection on the Journey: Encourage readers to reflect on their own journey, the challenges they've overcome, and how their faith has guided them.

Closing

- Final Thoughts: Summarize the central theme of the chapter, which is the importance of navigating dating challenges while staying true to your Christian faith.
    - Reflection Questions: Provide a set of reflection questions for readers to contemplate and discuss, helping them apply the principles of faith, values, and perseverance in their dating lives.

Chapter 4, "Navigating Challenges and Staying True to Faith," delves into the common obstacles and difficulties that can arise in Christian dating. It offers practical guidance on overcoming these challenges, staying true to one's values, and finding inspiration in faith to navigate the complexities of dating.

5

Cultivating Love and Commitment

Introduction
- Opening Quote: "Above all, love each other deeply, because love covers over a multitude of sins." – 1 Peter 4:8
- Recap of Previous Chapters: Begin by summarizing the key ideas explored in Chapters 1 through 4, particularly the importance of faith, connection, and overcoming challenges in Christian dating.

Section 1: The Nature of Love from a Christian Perspective

- Agape Love: Explain the concept of agape love, the selfless, unconditional love that is central to Christian teachings.
  - Love as a Choice: Discuss how love is not just a feeling but a conscious choice to act in love.
  - The Love of God: Reflect on how God's love serves as a model for human love in Christian relationships.

Section 2: The Stages of Love in Dating

- Friendship and Respect: Discuss the initial stages of friendship and respect that lay the foundation for deeper love.
   - Romantic Love: Explore the development of romantic feelings and how they can grow into lasting love.
   - Committed Love: Explain the importance of commitment in love and how it leads to a strong, enduring relationship.

Section 3: Cultivating Love in Christian Dating

- Acts of Love: Encourage readers to engage in acts of love and kindness to nurture the growth of love within the relationship.
   - Prayer and God's Guidance: Emphasize the role of prayer and seeking God's guidance to strengthen love and commitment.
   - Building a Christ-Centered Relationship: Discuss the significance of making Christ the center of the relationship and how it deepens love.

Section 4: Communication and Conflict Resolution in Love

- Effective Communication: Provide strategies for maintaining open, honest, and compassionate communication within the relationship.
   - Conflict as an Opportunity: Discuss how conflicts can be seen as opportunities to strengthen love and commitment.
   - Forgiveness in Love: Reiterate the importance of forgiveness in maintaining a loving and healthy relationship.

Section 5: Preparing for Lifelong Commitment

- Marriage as a Sacred Covenant: Explore the Christian perspective on marriage as a sacred covenant and commitment before God.
   - Pre-Marital Counseling: Explain the value of pre-marital counseling and how it can prepare couples for a lifetime of love and commitment.
   - The Role of Family and Community: Discuss the importance of involving family and the faith community in supporting the path to marriage.

Section 6: A Love That Lasts

- Success Stories: Share inspiring stories of Christian couples who have cultivated lasting love and commitment in their relationships.
    - Reflection on Love's Journey: Encourage readers to reflect on their own journey, how their love has grown, and how their faith has played a role.

Closing

- Final Thoughts: Summarize the central theme of the chapter, which is the cultivation of love and commitment within the context of Christian dating.
    - Reflection Questions: Provide a set of reflection questions for readers to contemplate and discuss, helping them apply the principles of love, commitment, and faith in their dating lives.

Chapter 5, "Cultivating Love and Commitment," focuses on the growth of love in Christian dating relationships. It emphasizes the Christian perspective on love, the importance of commitment, and the nurturing of love through communication, conflict resolution, and the support of the faith community.

6

The Decision to Commit

Introduction

- Opening Quote: "Two are better than one because they have a good return for their labor." – Ecclesiastes 4:9

- Recap of Previous Chapters: Start by summarizing the key concepts discussed in Chapters 1 to 5, with a focus on faith, connection, love, and commitment in Christian dating.

Section 1: Preparing for a Lifelong Commitment

- The Covenant of Marriage: Discuss the significance of marriage as a covenant before God and the lifelong commitment it represents.

- Understanding Commitment: Explain what commitment means in the context of a Christian relationship, emphasizing its enduring nature.

- Readiness for Commitment: Discuss the indicators of readiness for a lifelong commitment, including emotional and spiritual preparedness.

Section 2: Discernment and Decision-Making

- Seeking God's Will: Emphasize the importance of seeking God's guidance in making the decision to commit to a particular relationship.

- Prayer and Discernment: Offer practical advice on prayer and discernment to help readers make an informed choice.

- Overcoming Doubt: Discuss how to overcome doubts and uncertainty when deciding on commitment.

Section 3: Signs of a Healthy and Christ-Centered Relationship

- Mutual Respect and Support: Discuss the importance of mutual respect and support in a Christ-centered relationship.

- Shared Values and Goals: Emphasize the alignment of values and life goals as indicators of a healthy relationship.

- Communication and Conflict Resolution: Highlight effective communication and conflict resolution as signs of relationship strength.

Section 4: Making the Commitment Official

- Engagement and Marriage Preparation: Discuss the period of engagement and the value of pre-marital counseling in preparing for marriage.

- Ceremony and Vows: Explore the significance of the marriage ceremony and the exchange of vows before God.

- Legal and Practical Considerations: Offer guidance on the legal and practical aspects of marriage preparation.

Section 5: Building a Christ-Centered Marriage

- Spiritual Leadership: Discuss the role of spiritual leadership in a Christian marriage, with both partners supporting each other's faith journey.

- Love and Service: Emphasize the importance of love, selflessness, and service in a Christ-centered marriage.

- Maintaining Connection: Offer strategies for maintaining the connection, love, and commitment in a marriage.

Section 6: A Lifelong Journey of Love and Faith

- Life Together: Discuss the lifelong journey of a Christian marriage, with its joys, challenges, and opportunities for growth.
    - Stories of Enduring Love: Share inspirational stories of Christian couples whose commitment and faith have sustained them through the years.
    - Reflection on Your Commitment: Encourage readers to reflect on their own journey and the decisions they've made in their pursuit of lasting love and faith.

Closing

- Final Thoughts: Summarize the key takeaways from the chapter, emphasizing the significance of the decision to commit within a Christian context.
    - Reflection Questions: Provide a set of reflection questions for readers to contemplate and discuss, helping them apply the principles of commitment, discernment, and faith in their dating and relationship journey.

Chapter 6, "The Decision to Commit," explores the final steps in the journey of Christian dating: the commitment to marriage. It guides readers in discerning whether a relationship is suitable for a lifelong commitment, offers advice on making that commitment official, and discusses the key aspects of building a Christ-centered marriage.

7

Nurturing Lasting Love

Introduction

- Opening Quote: "And over all these virtues put on love, which binds them all together in perfect unity." – Colossians 3:14

- Recap of Previous Chapters: Begin by summarizing the key concepts discussed in Chapters 1 to 6, with a focus on faith, connection, love, commitment, and marriage within the context of Christian dating.

Section 1: The Journey Beyond the Wedding Day

- The Transition to Marriage: Discuss the transition from dating and engagement to married life and the adjustments it entails.

- Understanding Lasting Love: Explain the concept of lasting love and the factors that contribute to a strong, enduring marriage.

- The Role of Faith: Emphasize how faith continues to be the foundation for nurturing love in marriage.

Section 2: Building a Christ-Centered Home

- Creating a Christ-Centered Environment: Discuss the importance of making Christ the center of the home, with prayer, devotion, and faith practices.

- Shared Spiritual Growth: Explore the idea of mutual spiritual growth within a marriage, where both partners support and nurture each other's faith.

- Raising Children in Faith: Address the significance of imparting Christian values to children and maintaining a faith-centered family.

Section 3: Communication and Conflict Resolution in Marriage

- Continued Communication: Discuss the need for ongoing, open, and effective communication within a marriage.

- Navigating Conflict as a Team: Offer strategies for resolving conflicts and challenges as a united and faith-centered team.

- Forgiveness and Grace: Reiterate the importance of forgiveness, grace, and empathy in a Christian marriage.

Section 4: Shared Goals and Dreams

- Setting Shared Goals: Emphasize the value of establishing shared goals and dreams as a couple, both in terms of faith and life aspirations.

- Supporting Each Other's Callings: Discuss how partners can support and encourage each other's individual callings, whether they be related to work, ministry, or personal growth.

- Planning for the Future: Address the importance of future planning and preparation for the years ahead, including retirement and elder care.

Section 5: Growing Together in Love and Faith

- Nurturing Romance: Discuss the importance of nurturing romance and maintaining a deep emotional connection within the marriage.

- Celebrating Milestones and Traditions: Highlight the significance of celebrating important milestones and faith-based traditions.

- Serving Others as a Couple: Encourage readers to consider how they can serve others together as a couple, both within the faith community and in the broader world.

Section 6: Lifelong Love and Faith

- The Journey Continues: Discuss how the journey of love and faith in a Christian marriage is an ongoing, lifelong process.
  - Inspiring Love Stories: Share inspiring stories of Christian couples who have nurtured lasting love and faith through the years.
  - Reflection on Your Journey: Encourage readers to reflect on their own journey, the growth of their love and faith, and their hopes for the future.

Closing

- Final Thoughts: Summarize the key takeaways from the chapter, emphasizing the importance of nurturing lasting love and faith in a Christian marriage.
  - Reflection Questions: Provide a set of reflection questions for readers to contemplate and discuss, helping them apply the principles of lasting love, faith, and commitment in their own marriages.

Chapter 7, "Nurturing Lasting Love," explores the journey of love and faith beyond the wedding day, within the context of a Christian marriage. It provides guidance on building a Christ-centered home, maintaining effective communication, setting shared goals, and continuing to grow together in love and faith through the years.

8

Love that Endures

Introduction
- Opening Quote: "Love never fails." – 1 Corinthians 13:8
- Recap of Previous Chapters: Begin by summarizing the key concepts discussed in Chapters 1 to 7, focusing on the journey of faith, connection, love, commitment, and nurturing lasting love within Christian relationships.

Section 1: The Power of God's Love

- God's Unconditional Love: Discuss the profound impact of God's unconditional love on human relationships and how it serves as a model for enduring love.
- Love as a Witness to Faith: Explain how the love within Christian relationships can be a testimony to God's presence and work in our lives.

Section 2: Overcoming Challenges and Trials

- Navigating Life's Challenges: Address the various challenges that couples may face over the years, such as health issues, financial struggles, and personal crises.

- Faith as an Anchor: Emphasize how faith can provide strength and resilience in the face of adversity and serve as a source of hope and comfort.

Section 3: Renewing Love in Marriage

- Rekindling the Flame: Discuss the importance of rekindling the romance and passion in a marriage, even after many years together.
  - Date Nights and Getaways: Offer practical ideas for keeping the love alive through date nights and occasional getaways.
  - Celebrating Milestones: Encourage couples to celebrate milestones and anniversaries as reminders of their enduring love.

Section 4: Sharing Wisdom and Experience

- Mentoring and Ministry: Discuss how experienced couples can mentor younger ones and become involved in marriage and relationship ministry within the faith community.
  - Passing on Wisdom: Encourage the sharing of wisdom and lessons learned from a lifelong marriage with others.
  - Legacy of Love: Explore the concept of leaving a legacy of love and faith for future generations.

Section 5: Faith and Love in Later Life

- Embracing Aging Together: Discuss the unique challenges and opportunities of aging as a couple and the importance of supporting each other through these phases.
  - Spiritual Reflection: Encourage couples to engage in spiritual reflection and contemplation as they approach the later stages of life.

Section 6: The Journey Continues: Looking Forward with Faith and Love

- Retirement and New Adventures: Explore how retirement can be a time for new adventures, shared hobbies, and travel.

- Reinvesting in the Faith Community: Discuss the potential for couples to reinvest in their faith community and engage in volunteer and ministry work.

- Continuing to Grow Together: Emphasize that the journey of faith and love never truly ends; it is a lifelong process of growth and renewal.

Closing

- Final Thoughts: Summarize the key takeaways from the chapter, highlighting the enduring nature of love and faith within a Christian relationship.

- Reflection Questions: Provide a set of reflection questions for readers to contemplate and discuss, encouraging them to apply the principles of enduring love and faith in their own relationships and marriages.

Chapter 8, "Love that Endures," explores the lifelong journey of love and faith within Christian relationships, including the power of God's love, overcoming challenges, renewing love, sharing wisdom, and embracing the later stages of life. It reinforces the idea that love and faith continue to grow and thrive throughout a lifetime.

9

A Love that Transcends

Introduction
- Opening Quote: "There is no fear in love. But perfect love drives out fear." – 1 John 4:18
- Recap of Previous Chapters: Start by summarizing the key concepts discussed in Chapters 1 to 8, with a focus on the enduring nature of love and faith in Christian relationships.

Section 1: Love Beyond This World

- Eternal Love: Discuss the concept of love that transcends the temporal and extends into the eternal, as a reflection of God's unending love.
- The Connection Between Earthly and Divine Love: Explore how earthly love can be a glimpse of the divine and serve as a bridge to a deeper understanding of God's love.

Section 2: Faith, Hope, and Love

- Theological Virtues: Discuss the theological virtues of faith, hope, and love

as the core principles that guide Christian relationships.
   - The Role of Hope: Emphasize the importance of hope in sustaining love and faith, even in challenging times.
   - Love as the Greatest: Reiterate the biblical teaching that love is the greatest of these virtues.

Section 3: Serving Together in Faith and Love

- Servant Leadership: Discuss the idea of both partners adopting a role of servant leadership in the relationship, reflecting Christ's example.
   - Ministry and Community Service: Explore the potential for couples to serve together in ministries and community service, extending their love and faith to others.

Section 4: Navigating Loss and Grief

- Coping with Loss: Address the challenges of dealing with loss and grief, whether it's the loss of loved ones or the difficulties of life.
   - Supporting Each Other: Offer guidance on how couples can support each other in times of grief, drawing strength from their shared faith and love.

Section 5: Passing the Torch of Faith and Love

- Mentoring and Discipleship: Discuss the importance of mentoring and discipleship in the context of relationships and faith.
   - Transmitting Values: Encourage couples to actively transmit their values, faith, and love to the next generation.
   - Leaving a Legacy of Love: Explore the idea of leaving a legacy of love, faith, and service to the world.

Section 6: The Journey Continues: Love Beyond Measure

- Continued Growth and Renewal: Emphasize that love and faith continue to grow and renew throughout life, transcending the boundaries of time.

- Reflection on the Journey: Encourage readers to reflect on their own journey, how their love and faith have transcended challenges, and the legacy they hope to leave.

Closing

- Final Thoughts: Summarize the key takeaways from the chapter, emphasizing the transcendent nature of love and faith in Christian relationships.

- Reflection Questions: Provide a set of reflection questions for readers to contemplate and discuss, helping them apply the principles of transcendent love and faith in their own lives and relationships.

Chapter 9, "A Love that Transcends," delves into the profound and enduring aspects of love and faith within Christian relationships. It explores the idea of love that goes beyond this world, the theological virtues of faith, hope, and love, serving together, coping with loss, passing on values, and leaving a legacy of love and faith that transcends time and circumstances.

10

A Love That Inspires

Introduction

- Opening Quote: "Let us love one another, for love comes from God." – 1 John 4:7

- Recap of Previous Chapters: Begin by summarizing the key concepts discussed in Chapters 1 to 9, with an emphasis on the enduring and transcendent nature of love and faith in Christian relationships.

Section 1: The Power of Testimony

- Sharing Your Love Story: Discuss the significance of sharing your love story as a testimony to others, showing how faith and love have shaped your journey.

- Inspiring Others: Explain how your love story can inspire others in their own dating and relationship experiences.

Section 2: The Impact of a Christ-Centered Relationship

- A Light to the World: Explore how a Christ-centered relationship can shine as a beacon of hope and love in the world, even amid challenging times.

- Counteracting Negative Influences: Discuss how your relationship can be a counterbalance to negative cultural influences on dating and love.

Section 3: Nurturing Faith and Love in the Community

- Community Involvement: Encourage couples to actively participate in their faith community, supporting and nurturing faith and love in others.

- Mentoring and Counseling: Discuss how couples can become mentors and counselors, guiding others in their own relationships and faith journeys.

Section 4: The Journey of Love and Faith as a Ministry

- Relationship Ministry: Explore the concept of making your journey of love and faith a ministry, serving others by sharing your experiences and wisdom.

- Teaching and Speaking: Discuss the potential for couples to teach and speak about Christian relationships and dating at conferences, workshops, or within the church.

Section 5: Overcoming the Challenges of Modern Dating

- Addressing Contemporary Issues: Discuss how couples can address modern dating challenges with a Christian perspective, offering guidance and support to singles.

- Online Presence: Explore the responsible use of social media and online platforms to spread positive messages about faith-centered dating and love.

Section 6: The Never-Ending Journey: Love as a Legacy

- Eternal Impact: Emphasize that the impact of your love and faith journey is not limited by time but extends into eternity.

- Reflection on Your Legacy: Encourage readers to reflect on the legacy they want to leave in terms of faith, love, and inspiration to future generations.

Closing

- Final Thoughts: Summarize the key takeaways from the chapter, focusing on the potential for a Christ-centered relationship to inspire and impact others.
  - Reflection Questions: Provide a set of reflection questions for readers to contemplate and discuss, helping them consider how they can use their own love story to inspire and serve others.

Chapter 10, "A Love That Inspires," explores the potential for Christian couples to inspire and impact others through their love story and journey of faith. It emphasizes the power of testimony, the influence of Christ-centered relationships, the importance of nurturing faith and love in the community, and the idea of turning one's love story into a ministry to benefit others.

11

A Future Filled with Faith and Love

Introduction

- Opening Quote: "For I know the plans I have for you, declares the Lord, plans to prosper you and not to harm you, plans to give you hope and a future." – Jeremiah 29:11

- Recap of Previous Chapters: Start by summarizing the key concepts discussed in Chapters 1 to 10, with a focus on the enduring and inspiring nature of love and faith in Christian relationships.

Section 1: Embracing the Unknown Future

- Trusting God's Plan: Discuss the importance of trusting God's plan for your future, both as individuals and as a couple.

- Navigating Uncertainty: Address the uncertainties that may come with planning for the future, and the role of faith in facing these unknowns.

Section 2: Family Planning and Parenthood

- Building a Family: Explore the topic of family planning, discussing how faith can guide decisions about when and how to start a family.

- Christian Parenting: Share insights on how to raise children with Christian values and principles.

- Balancing Work and Family: Discuss strategies for balancing careers, family life, and faith.

Section 3: Building a Christ-Centered Home

- Cultivating a Spiritual Environment: Discuss the significance of creating a Christ-centered atmosphere in your home, with regular devotion and prayer.

- Raising Children in Faith: Emphasize the importance of teaching children about Christianity, the Bible, and moral values.

- Fostering Love and Unity: Address how couples can maintain a loving and unified family environment.

Section 4: Nurturing Love Through the Seasons

- Adapting to Change: Discuss how couples can adapt to the changes and challenges that different life stages bring.

- Rekindling Romance: Offer practical tips for keeping the romance alive through the years.

- Reinvesting in the Relationship: Emphasize the importance of continuously investing in the relationship to keep the love and faith strong.

Section 5: Supporting Each Other's Callings

- Individual and Shared Callings: Explore the idea of supporting each other's unique callings and aspirations, whether they relate to work, ministry, or personal growth.

- Encouraging Personal Development: Discuss the role of encouraging personal growth and development within the relationship.

- Balancing Priorities: Provide guidance on balancing personal callings with family and relationship priorities.

Section 6: The Journey Continues: Hope and Faith for the Future

- Hope for the Future: Discuss the hopes and dreams that you and your partner have for your future together.
  - Continued Growth and Renewal: Emphasize that the journey of love and faith is ongoing, with new adventures and opportunities for growth.
  - Reflection on the Journey: Encourage readers to reflect on their own journey, their dreams for the future, and the role of faith and love in shaping their path.

Closing

- Final Thoughts: Summarize the key takeaways from the chapter, focusing on the role of faith and love in shaping a hopeful future.
  - Reflection Questions: Provide a set of reflection questions for readers to contemplate and discuss, helping them consider their own plans for a future filled with faith and love.

Chapter 11, "A Future Filled with Faith and Love," explores the journey of love and faith as couples plan for their future. It addresses family planning, creating a Christ-centered home, nurturing love through the years, supporting each other's callings, and the hope and faith that guide their future.

12

A Love That Endures Eternally

Introduction
- Opening Quote: "So now faith, hope, and love abide, these three; but the greatest of these is love." – 1 Corinthians 13:13
- Recap of Previous Chapters: Begin by summarizing the key concepts discussed in Chapters 1 to 11, with a focus on the enduring and inspiring nature of love and faith in Christian relationships.

Section 1: The Everlasting Love of God

- God's Eternal Love: Discuss the eternal and unwavering love of God as the foundation of all human love.
- The Connection Between Earthly and Divine Love: Explore how earthly love is a reflection of God's love and has the potential to endure eternally.

Section 2: The Promises of Marriage

- Marriage as a Covenant: Reiterate the concept of marriage as a sacred covenant before God, bound by promises of love, faithfulness, and support.

- Vows and Commitments: Discuss the role of vows and commitments in marriage, emphasizing their enduring nature.
- The Legacy of Marriage: Explore how a loving and faithful marriage can leave a lasting legacy for generations to come.

Section 3: Love and Faith Through Life's Trials

- Trials and Tests: Address how love and faith can guide couples through life's trials, including illness, financial difficulties, and loss.
- Staying United in Adversity: Discuss the importance of staying united and faithful in the face of challenges.
- The Role of Prayer and Faith: Emphasize how prayer and faith provide strength and hope in times of hardship.

Section 4: Passing the Torch of Faith and Love

- Mentoring and Discipleship: Discuss the significance of mentoring and discipleship in the context of faith and relationships.
- Transmitting Values: Encourage couples to actively transmit their values, faith, and love to the next generation.
- Leaving a Legacy of Love: Explore the idea of leaving a legacy of love, faith, and service for the world.

Section 5: A Love that Goes Beyond Time

- Eternal Impact: Emphasize that the impact of a loving and faithful relationship is not limited by time but extends into eternity.
- Reflection on Your Legacy: Encourage readers to reflect on the legacy they want to leave, both within their family and the broader community.

Section 6: Living in the Fullness of Love and Faith

- A Love That Continues: Discuss the idea that love and faith continue to grow and endure eternally, transcending the boundaries of time and space.

- Hope for the Future: Explore the hopes and dreams that couples have for their love and faith as they continue their journey together.

- The Everlasting Journey: Emphasize that the journey of love and faith is a lifelong, eternal adventure.

Closing

- Final Thoughts: Summarize the key takeaways from the chapter, focusing on the concept of a love that endures eternally and the role of faith in shaping this love.

- Reflection Questions: Provide a set of reflection questions for readers to contemplate and discuss, helping them consider their own journey of love and faith that transcends time and continues into eternity.

Chapter 12, "A Love That Endures Eternally," explores the eternal nature of love and faith within the context of Christian relationships. It emphasizes the role of God's eternal love, the promises of marriage, navigating trials, passing on values, and the idea of leaving a legacy of love and faith that goes beyond time.

Book Summary: Divine Dating: A Christian Perspective on Finding Love

"Divine Dating" is a heartfelt and insightful guide that navigates the intricate journey of finding love through the lens of Christian faith. This book serves as a companion for those seeking meaningful, enduring relationships grounded in the principles of Christianity.

The book is divided into twelve chapters, each offering a unique perspective and practical advice on the various aspects of Christian dating and building a Christ-centered relationship.

Chapter 1: Foundations of Faith in Dating

The journey begins with establishing a solid foundation of faith, emphasizing the importance of spiritual connection as the cornerstone of a loving partnership.

Chapter 2: The Power of Connection

Building on the foundation of faith, Chapter 2 delves into the significance of meaningful connections and provides guidance on forming authentic relationships.

Chapter 3: Discerning God's Will in Love

Chapter 3 explores the concept of discernment, teaching readers how to seek God's guidance in their dating journey, ensuring their path aligns with His divine plan.

Chapter 4: Navigating Challenges and Staying True to Faith

This chapter delves into common challenges in faith-centered dating and offers strategies for overcoming them while remaining true to Christian values.

Chapter 5: Cultivating Love and Commitment

Readers learn how to cultivate love and commitment within a Christian relationship, exploring the stages of love and practical steps to nurture a lasting connection.

Chapter 6: The Decision to Commit

Chapter 6 guides readers through the decision to commit to marriage, discussing the importance of readiness and the role of faith in this significant step.

Chapter 7: Nurturing Lasting Love

This chapter focuses on nurturing love within the context of marriage. It delves into creating a Christ-centered home, effective communication, and conflict resolution.

Chapter 8: Love that Endures

Chapter 8 explores the enduring and transcendent nature of love within Christian relationships, addressing family planning, raising children in faith, and maintaining love through the seasons of life.

Chapter 9: A Love that Inspires

In Chapter 9, readers discover how their love story can inspire others, and they are encouraged to support faith and love within their community.

Chapter 10: A Future Filled with Faith and Love

Readers learn how to plan their future with faith and love in mind, addressing family planning, balancing work and family, and nurturing love through life's trials.

Chapter 11: A Love That Transcends

Chapter 11 discusses love that transcends time and circumstances, exploring the impact of love beyond the earthly realm and the power of sharing one's love story.

Chapter 12: A Love That Endures Eternally

The final chapter emphasizes the eternal nature of love and faith. It discusses the legacy of marriage, passing on values, and the everlasting impact of a Christ-centered relationship.

"Divine Dating" offers valuable insights, practical advice, and thought-provoking reflections for those seeking love in alignment with Christian values. It reinforces the idea that love, when rooted in faith, is not only enduring but also transcends time and circumstances, leaving a lasting legacy for generations to come. This book serves as a beacon of hope and inspiration for those on the journey to find love within the Christian faith.

www.ingramcontent.com/pod-product-compliance
Lightning Source LLC
LaVergne TN
LVHW010439070526
838199LV00066B/6089